Patricia Nicole Harris
WRITTEN BY

JèTaun
ILLUSTRATED BY

Charly Evon Simpson
& Arlani Chanel Harris
EDITED BY

Copyright © 2021 Cam And Lex Adventures
ISBN 978-1-7373628-0-7

CAM

LEX

DEDICATED TO

My nephew and godson **Camden Lorenzo** (the big cousin)
and my son **Lexington Grey** (the little cousin).

Although you are cousins, may you two
continue to love one another, protect one
another, and go through this adventure called
life as brothers and besties for all eternity.
I love you both as my own and you make life
so much fun.

#BrotherCousins

Our daughter **Savannah Renee** who has
stolen all our hearts, especially those of her
big brother and big cousin.

#SisterCousin

Our angel baby who is always
on our mind and in our hearts

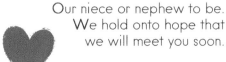

Our niece or nephew to be.
We hold onto hope that
we will meet you soon.

All of my cousins who contribute to my life's
greatest memories.

ADDITIONAL THANKS TO

My amazingly supportive husband **Farrin**.

My sister **Tammy** who so bravely brought Camden into this word.

My Wingman/Brother–in law **Taurean**. Thanks for letting me turn your kid into a cartoon!

David Heredia. Thank you for believing in me and coaching me through this journey and inspiring me with your #HeroesOfColor story.

All of my friends and family that took time to share their own cousinly love stories with me.

Finally, thank you to **our parents and grandparents** whose love and devotion to one another started it all. These adventures are possible because of you.

VISIT US FOR MORE RESOURCES AND FUN
www. CamAndLexAdventures .com

Cam and Lex are the best of friends. They do everything together it's true. Their mommies are sisters, so what does that mean? You are right! They are cousins too.

Cam and Lex have a special bond.
One that will last forever.

Keep turning the pages so we can join Cam and Lex on all of
their fun adventures!

Cam is the oldest. He likes to play ball, dance, and sing.

Lex is into superheroes and puzzles are his thing.

They are both different and do things their own way. But there is nothing they enjoy more than being together each day.

Let the adventures begin!

Cam and Lex go on road trips. They like to play "I spy."
Cam spots something GREEN and what
does Lex see?

Look up there in the sky!

Cam and Lex go camping. They want to go again soon. They make s'mores by the fire and when they get tired, they sleep under stars and the moon.

Cam and Lex go swimming. They swim all day like fish. Cam says to Lex "Come on cousin! You can do it! Just kick your legs like this."

Cam and Lex use their imagination. Things are not what they seem. A stick is a magic wand and a box becomes a time machine!

Cam and Lex go to school! They love learning about volcanoes and space.

In his class, Cam won "friend of the month" and Lex knows all of his shapes!

Cam and Lex visit their Grands.
Aren't Grandparents the greatest?! They watch movies, play games
like hide and go seek, and see who can stay up the latest.

Cam and Lex are pajama chefs! Family recipes they like to try. They wear matching PJ's and bake lots of treats like cakes and peach cobbler pie.

Cam and Lex have a sleepover every chance they get. They make a mess and act silly and it is one of their favorite adventures yet!

Cam and Lex welcome their sister and cousin.
Her name is Savannah Renee. She is little for now but when she gets
bigger, she will join in and play.

Cam and Lex dream big! They explore who they want to be.
What will they become? They can be whatever they want.
We just have to wait and see!

Cam and Lex always find something to do. All they need is each other. It is so much fun having a cousin who is just like a sister or brother.

There are times Cam and Lex do not get along and they are not having the best day.

Feelings get hurt, they need time apart,
but everything will be okay.

They say "I'm sorry." They forgive and forget, and they always continue to play.

No matter what, they hug and make up, because the next big adventure awaits!

To my readers,

Thank you for your support. My prayer is that this book brings joy to every home it may enter.

Please post your: #CousinlyLove #BrotherCousins #SisterCousins #SiblingCousins #SiblingLove pictures

And tag our handle

@CamAndLexAdventures
for a feature on our Instagram page.

We want to bear witness to all the adventure that exists between those who are growing up together, related by blood, friendship, and love.

Visit us for more resources and fun
www.CamAndLexAdventures.com

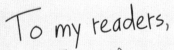